AN ADDRESS

DELIVERED AT THE FAIR OF THE AMERICAN INSTITUTE, NEW-YORK CITY,

OCTOBER 13, 1870.

BY JOHN L. HAYES,

SECRETARY OF THE NATIONAL ASSOCIATION OF WOOL MANUFACTURERS.

CAMBRIDGE:

PRESS OF JOHN WILSON AND SON.

1870.

THE SOLIDARITY OF THE INDUSTRIES
AS ILLUSTRATED BY THE RELATIONS OF THE WOOLLEN MANUFACTURE.

An Address delivered at the Fair of the American Institute, New York City, Oct. 13, 1870. BY JOHN L. HAYES.

IN presence of hese magnificent products of a diversified native industry, at the same time evidences of national progress and inspirations for higher achievements, it would be a waste of words to dwell upon the importance of sustaining upon our soil the general industry which has placed before our eyes these brilliant results. The duty of developing a national industry is not a question for argument; it is a sentiment like patriotism or filial love, and here, at least, we could find few who will not agree with the greatest of living geologists, Elie de Beaumont, that "of all the tendencies which occupy different civilized nations, the most marked is that of fixing upon their own territory all those branches of industrial activity which suit its soil, climate, and commercial position; and that government will most preserve the respect of neighboring nations, and show itself worthy of the respect of its people, which shall use all its means of action to favor with discernment this tendency." And few would refuse to partake of the "noble emulation of producing every thing," which the venerable Thiers says is possessed by all intelligent and free nations.

"What, then," says he, "are the nations which have sought to develop among themselves a national labor?"

"They are the nations which are intelligent and free. When the foreigner brings them a product, after they have found it serviceable, they desire to undertake it. The nations which do not have this desire are the indolent nations of the East; intelligent and free nations seek to appropriate for themselves the products brought to them by foreign nations."

While the proposition of the importance of a diversified native industry, in the abstract, is generally accepted, the favors which special industries demand from national legislation are frequently the subject of condemnation. We have seen quite recently the copper, the iron, the steel, the woollen, the salt industries, each reproached for the special consideration which they have invoked in legislation. Appearing before you as the representative of a special industry, I offer the apology for my position, and find the guiding thread for my remarks, in the subject to which I now beg your attention,— *The Solidarity of the Industries, as Illustrated by the Relations of the Woollen Manufacture.* An eminent liberal statesman, who now occupies a place in the new government of France, Jules Simon, closes a recent free-trade speech in the Legislative Assembly by the transcendental remark, "All the liberties are sisters: if we have liberty of trade, we shall have all the others." This remark is only sentimental nonsense, for there is no necessary relation, except in words, between free trade and free government; but, slightly changed, it expresses what I mean by the solidarity of industries. *All the industries are sisters: if we have one, we shall have all the others.*

Let me at the outset exclude the inference that the woollen manufacture is not of itself, and independently of its relations to other interests, of the highest national importance. A manufacture whose direct annual product in the United States is, by the most careful estimates, of the value of one hundred and seventy-five million dollars, making necessary an importation of only sixty-five millions, thus supplying nearly three-quarters of the whole consumption of woollen and worsted goods in the country; which employs directly at least one hundred and twenty thousand operatives, and supports twice as many more; which consumes the fleeces of thirty-five million sheep; which supplies with cheap and sound clothing the great mass of the people, furnishing nearly all the cassimeres, tricots, and cheviots, for business suits; the beavers, moscows, and cloakings, for outer garments; the knit goods for under-clothing, and the flannels and blankets for bed-coverings; which furnishes all the ingrain carpets consumed here, produced from twice the number of looms that are in England, making the American working-man's parlor and bedroom the most cheerful and attractive that labor ever found for repose; a manufacture which supplies all our delaines, the most largely consumed of the cheaper fabrics for woman's wear; which is daily producing new fabrics for female attire, such as worsted poplins, serges, cloakings, printed cashmeres, alpaca and mohair lustres; a manufacture which furnishes lastings for our shoes, enough for thirty thousand a week in a single establishment, reducing the price of the foreign article in two years from $1.10 to 66 cents a yard; which supplies for our furniture all-wool and union damasks, silk cotelines and reps of tasteful designs and beautiful colors; an industry which has torn down the British bunting, which has so long disgraced our national ships, and has run up a real American flag made of our own wools and in our own mills, — a flag which means not merely political, but industrial independence; a manufacture which in the last five years has made more progress than in any twenty years before, and more than any other branch of textile industry has done, and which by its own grand exhibition in this hall last year won the reluctant admiration of your shrewd importers, and the generous admiration of a diplomatic representative of Great Britain, — an industry like this, I say, has claims of itself alone for grateful appreciation by the American people, and for vigorous defence by American legislators.

But I must hasten to a consideration of the indirect and less obvious influences of the woollen industry. And I must be permitted to go beyond our own country and the present time for my illustrations. Let me first show the relations of the wool manufacture to agriculture.

The woollen manufacture works up a fibre which was in primitive times, and is again becoming in quite recent times, the material of the first necessity for the clothing of man. This fibre outranks all others, — first, because it is made more perfect than any other, through the chemical elaborations of an animal of high organization, thus surpassing silk, which is derived from an animal of a lower organic structure. Again, its specific gravity being the least of all fibrous substances, its tissues are the lightest, warmest, and most healthful. And, finally, this material, provided in some varieties with a structure which enables the fibres to be laced and intermingled, by the process of fulling, into fabrics distinguished for their warmth and softness, in other varieties has a lustre which assimilates its tissues to those of silk; and, like silk, and unlike cotton and flax, it receives and permanently retains every tincture and every tone and hue which the art of the dyer can produce. The industrial application in primitive times of this marvellous material to clothing for man, in lieu of the skins of wild beasts, demanded the substitution of the pastoral system for that of the chase, and marked the first step of mankind in agriculture, and consequently in the way of civilization. The whole direct benefit to agriculture from the consumption of wool in manufactured products is measured by the annual value of the wool of the world, which is estimated by M. Moll, chairman of the jury on wools at the Paris Exposition, at three thousand million francs, or $600,000,000. The estimates of Mr. Lynch, approved by Mr. Bond, both high authorities, place the total wool clip of the United States, in 1868, at one hundred and seventy-seven million pounds. At forty cents per pound, the direct value of the American wool manufacture to American agriculture is nearly $71,000,000.

The direct is very far from the only or even chief benefit accruing to agriculture from the woollen industry. The Sheep, cultivated in primitive times, and at present in merely pastoral countries for only one of its aptitudes, that of producing wool, is found to have a more important aptitude, that of converting, in the shortest possible time, vegetable matter into the most healthful and nutritious flesh: and in countries most advanced in agriculture it has become the most important source of animal food. Again, wool, unlike tobacco, the cereals, the oleaginous seeds, and the vegetable textiles, including cotton, can, so far as is known, be produced and exported indefinitely without creating exhaustion of the soil; and even more than that, sheep, through the peculiar nutritiousness of their manure, and the facility with which it is distributed, are found to be the most economical and certain means of solving the highest problem in agriculture, — that of constantly renewing the productiveness of the land. Their manure is more valuable than that of cattle, because they digest better; they cut their food finer and chew it better. They void less vegetable fibre, and their excrements are more converted into soluble matter. "One thousand sheep, folded on an acre of ground one day, would manure it sufficiently to feed one thousand and one sheep. So that by this process, land which, the first year, can feed only one thousand sheep, may, the next year, as a result of their own droppings, feed thirteen hundred and sixty-five."

So said Anderson, more than forty years ago; and Sprengel allows that the manure of fourteen hundred sheep, for one day, is equal to manuring highly one acre of land, which is about four sheep per year. Mr. Mechi, a still more recent authority, estimates that fifteen hundred sheep folded on an acre of land for twenty-four hours, or one hundred sheep for fifteen days, would manure the land sufficiently to carry it through four years' rotation.

Permit me now to present in more detail some illustrations of the relations of the woollen industry to agriculture. I need not say that these relations are reciprocal. Action and reaction are equal in the moral as well as in the physical world. I have elsewhere shown the dependence of the manufacturers of each nation upon the wool-growers of their own country, and that the characteristic features of the manufactures of different nations have been impressed by the peculiar condition of their agriculture. I present the same picture, only with the point of view reversed. Manufactures instead of agriculture now occupy the foreground; and the latter, being in distant perspective, are made to appear subordinate to the latter.

The country where the woollen industry has had the longest standing, and the most complete development, naturally presents the most complete example of the interdependence upon which I insist. England, from a very early period, has produced sheep of two distinctly marked classes. The one class, thriving upon the dry uplands, produced a short, comparatively fine wool, adapted solely for making fulled cloths. Of this class the original Southdown was a type. This wool supplied the cloth manufactory established at Winchester in the time of the Romans. The other class of sheep, of greater size, flourishing upon the rich, moist plains, produced wool characterized by greater length, strength, and lustre, and its moderate felting properties. This wool, fitted for making serges and other stuff fabrics, adapted especially for female wear, was called combing wool, from the instrument used to make the fibres straight and parallel, preparatory to spinning. Until about the time of Elizabeth, England herself, worked up, the greater portion of her short wools into cloths; but exported nearly all her combing wools, far the most valuable of her agricultural products, which were made up into says and serges, by the workmen of the Low Countries. In the time of Elizabeth, the persecutions of the Duke of Alva drove the say weavers, skilled in working up the combing wools, from the Netherlands into England. The worsted manufacture, or that of the combing wools, was thus engrafted upon the industry of England, and prepared the way for the consumption of all her wools upon her own soil. The domestic consumption of all her wools was made a national necessity by stringent laws prohibiting the exportation of wool, which were in force from 1660 to 1825. The prohibition of exportation was especially efficacious in developing the worsted industry, as it compelled the manufacture at home of the combing wools formerly exported. The number of sheep during this period was nearly trebled, and the production of wool in each animal was doubled. As the worsted industry became developed, and agriculture became more prosperous, from the home markets opened for its products, the woollen industry and agriculture continued to react upon each other; the wool manufacture making increased demands for combing wool, or that produced by the heaviest sheep, and agriculture taking a direction to supply this demand.

In the mean time, the artificial or turnip husbandry was introduced by William of Orange, and the means were provided for trebling the number of sheep which an acre of land could support. The results at the present time to the English woollen manufacture are, that the worsted manufacture far surpasses the clothing-wool manufacture, the two together supporting a population of over a million; and the towns which have been the centres of the worsted manufacture have made a more rapid progress than any in Great Britain, Bradford having increased her population 90,000 in fifty years. The result of this reciprocal action to the agriculture of England is a genuine transformation, of external character at least, in the English races of sheep. The production of combing wool, the kind in greatest demand, was secured by breeding sheep which would attain the utmost possible weight of mutton, which could be fed to their utmost capacity, and would produce the utmost amount of manure. The merino sheep, although introduced into England at about the same time as into Germany and France, which they have so greatly enriched; and although their culture was encouraged by the King and the first noblemen of the realm, were finally wholly discarded. The mutton sheep is at this moment not only the chief animal product of England, but it is what it was declared to be long ago, "the sheet-anchor of English agriculture." It is the chief animal product of Great Britain. The statistics of domestic animals, published by the Royal Agricultural Society, show that Great Britain had, in 1868, 30,711,396 sheep, 5,423,981 cattle, and 2,308,539 pigs. The sheep is literally the basis of English husbandry. The agriculture of England, as a whole, is very simple. Four crops, in regular rotation and mainly in the same order, constitute her great staples. Turnips, barley, grass, and wheat, are said to be the four magical words at which the earth unlocks her treasures to the British farmer. The four field, or four shift system, which pervades the greater part of the kingdom, consists of this succession. The profit is in the barley and wheat alone; the turnips and grass serve mainly to feed the sheep, which furnish mutton and wool to support them in their most important function, that of manuring the turnip field upon which they are folded, for the four years' rotation. It is this function which I wish to bring into special prominence. Recent agricultural writers in England affirm this to be the main object of English sheep husbandry. Professor Coleman, of the Agricultural College of Cirencester, in a paper recently read before the Royal Agricultural Society, on the breeding and feeding of sheep, says: "It is not difficult to show that sheep alone, apart from their influence on the corn crops, will not pay a living profit, after all the expenses of growing the crops are considered." Other practical writers for the same journal declare that there is no profit in growing sheep in England simply for their mutton and wool, but that the culture of sheep is still an indispensable necessity, as there is no other means of keeping up the land.

Passing away from England, I observe that the highest authorities in France inculcate the same lesson. The most eminent of French practical statesmen, M. Thiers, in his great discourse on the protective question, delivered in the Legislative Assembly in January last, demands protective duties upon the wool of France; as it is threatened that the fine sheep, unprotected through duties on wool, must disappear from the soil of France, in consequence of competition from the southern hemisphere. He says: "Upon four-fifths of the territory, where the soil is stony, and only fine grasses abound, the fine sheep alone can convert this grass into flesh and manure." After giving the facts as to the decline of the ovine population of France, and its enormous increase in Australia and La Plata, he continues: "In this situation, how can the French resist the foreign competition? *The agricultural industry of France cannot dispense with sheep*. The facts which I have given you ought to inspire you with the most serious concern." The same lesson is taught by the best practical agriculturists of the United States. Mr. Stilson, president of the Wisconsin Wool-Growers' Association, has shown that his flock of fifteen hundred sheep has enabled him to produce eight or ten more bushels of wheat to the acre than is grown on the average lands of Wisconsin, where sheep husbandry is not an auxiliary to wheat farming. The president of the Ohio Wool-Growers' Association, Mr.

Stevens, whom I had the pleasure of meeting this summer, at the Indianapolis Exposition, assured me that he could see no means of reclaiming the rapidly deteriorating lands of Ohio except by the restorative influence of sheep husbandry. We have seen lands in certain portions of the West producing wheat so abundantly as to compel the opening of railroad lines for the single purpose of transporting their teeming harvests; and have also seen, in our own time, these very lands so rapidly exhausted, that the rails have been torn up for want of traffic. Such facts apprise us that there is no security for continued fruitfulness, even in our most fertile States, but in a more provident agriculture. What is taken from the land *must* be restored. Science gives us but little encouragement in the promise of cheap imported or artificial manures. The guano beds are being rapidly exhausted. The experiments of Messrs. Lawes and Gilbert, at Rothamsted, show that the application to the land of sewage from the cities, from which so much was expected, is a failure. The brilliant experiments of Vila, in France, made to exhibit the applicability of artificial manures in place of animal manures, in countries like France, where the land is so much divided as not to permit the profitable culture of animals, lead to no practical results, because no economical sources of artificial nitrates, phosphates, or potash, have been or are likely to be discovered. We see, but as through grated windows, exhaustless but practically inaccessible stores of potash in the granite rocks; of phosphates in beds of apatite; and of nitrogen in the atmosphere, or in the far-off rainless plains of Chili. Has not Providence locked up these treasures, or removed them from our reach, to compel man, for his highest physical good, to cultivate the animal which best supplies the primal necessities, — food, clothing, and the continued enrichment of the earth? The blessing, in the olden time, was given to him who "brought of the firstlings of his flock," for "the Lord had respect unto Abel and to his offering."

There are other relations of the woollen industry to agriculture, much less broad in their scope, but so interesting and illustrative that I cannot pass them by. The first which I allude to, because connected with the topic which we have just considered, is the achievement which chemical science has recently effected in saving the potash contained in the yolk of fleeces in such a form that it may be returned to the soil or used in the arts. It is well known that sheep draw from the land upon which they graze a considerable quantity of potash, which, after circulating in the blood, is excreted from the skin with the sweat, in combination with which it is deposited in the wool. The French chemists MM. Maumoné and Rogelet have established quite recently at the great seats of the woollen manufacture in France, as at Rheims and Elbeuf, factories for putting the new industry which they have created into practical operation. They induce the woollen manufacturers to preserve and sell to them the solutions of yolk obtained by the washing of the raw fleeces in cold water, and pay such a price as encourages the manufacturers to wash their wool methodically, so as to enrich the same water with the yolk of a number of fleeces. These scourings the chemists carry to their factory, and then boil them down to a dry, carbonaceous residuum. The alkaline salts remain in the charred residuum, and are extracted by lixiviation with water. The most important of the alkalies obtained is potash, which is recovered in a state of great purity. It is computed that if the fleeces of all the sheep of France, estimated at forty-seven millions, were subjected to the new treatment, France would derive from this source alone all the potash she requires in the arts, enough to make about twelve thousand tons of commercial carbonate of potash, convertible into seventeen thousand five hundred tons of saltpetre, which would charge eighteen hundred and seventy million cartridges. So that the inoffensive sheep, the emblem of peace, can be made to supply the chief muniment of war. The obvious lesson from these facts, to the sheep farmer, is to wash his fleeces at home, in such a manner that the wash water, so rich in potash, may be distributed upon the land as liquid manure.

I have already adverted to the influence of the wool manufacture of England in developing the breeds of long-woolled sheep in that country. Facts illustrative of the influence of manufacture upon sheep husbandry are furnished by all manufacturing nations.

In the indolent nations of the East, manufacturers adapt themselves to the raw material which has been furnished for ages. The beautiful Turkish carpets of Asia Minor are produced now, as they doubtless were in the time of the Crusades, from coarse wool grown upon the Barbarous broad-tailed sheep, which is still precisely the same as those which formed the flocks watched by the shepherds of the Bible, and to which belonged the Paschal lamb. Nations of higher civilization are constantly varying their fabric and their sheep husbandry.

The Spanish merino, which I conceive to be a relic of Greek and Roman civilization preserved in the mountains of Andalusia from the barbarians who swept over most of the Roman possessions, was introduced about a century ago into all the manufacturing nations of Europe. When introduced into France, at the sheep-folds of Rambouillet, it produced a short clothing wool. Let me, before describing the important change which subsequently took place, advert for a moment to a zoölogical principle.

A beautiful law of nature has been brought into view by the studies of modern zoölogy, that, while the primary and specific characters, determined by the forms of the skeleton, are absolutely fixed, and transmit themselves infallibly by generation, the secondary or accessory forms of animals, such as the fleshy covering, hair, and fleece, the only characters which man has in view in cultivating the domestic animals, can be modified indefinitely by culture. For example, the sheep in a state of nature is provided with two kinds of covering. The outer or principal covering is a coarse hair. Beneath this hair, and concealed by it, is a short, fine down. It is this down, which, by the culture of sheep in a state of domestication, has become the woolly fleece, and which is again susceptible of being modified by the climate in which it is developed, or the care of which it is the object. This modification of the secondary characters of animals is sometimes the result of high agricultural skill, or, to use the more accurate modern term, *zootechnic* skill, directed to a specific object, as in the labors of Bakewell and Elman, in England, and of Hammond, in Vermont. But the modification generally takes place insensibly.

One of the most important of these insensible influences is that which the wool manufacture exerts in its demand for the material for its fabrics. The merino, as I have observed, when introduced into France was a small, short-woolled sheep. The higher feeding naturally given to the precious animals necessarily tended to increase the size, and at the same time to lengthen the fibre, it being the fixed law that woolly fibre is increased in length but not in diameter by increased nourishment. French industry, with that creative genius which is its highest attribute, saw in the newly acquired fibre a means for creating new, soft fabrics for female wear, in place of the coarse and stiff serges which were the characteristic stuffs of the former country. Here was a fresh raw material for the novelties in dress which the world of fashion is perpetually calling upon France to supply. Remember that before the present century no female stuffs were made of fine wool. In 1801, Dauphinot Pallotan invented the most beautiful of all woollen tissues, the *French merino*, at present, or recently, the chief product of Rheims and its fifty thousand workmen, and the sole product of a single establishment at Cateau, with ten thousand workmen. In 1826, M. Jourdain invented all-wool *mousselines de laines* for printing, the material being long merino fleece. In 1838, he created *challis*, a fabric with a warp of silk organzine and a weft of merino wool. Since then the dress fabrics of which merino wool forms the chief component material have been infinitely varied to meet the insatiable demands of fashion for change. The Exposition of 1867 demonstrated that of all the fabrics which the art of man has produced, there are none which bear comparison in tastefulness, variety, and perfection of workmanship, with the French dress tissues of merino wool.

The demands of the wool industry of France gradually and insensibly converted the fibre of her merinos into a combing wool. The wool could not be made to acquire the length required for combing without increasing the size of the animal. The merinos of France are the largest animals of their race in the world. They are said to be, as compared with the American merino, bred for a different purpose, "what the great, pampered shorthorn of England is to the little, hardy, black cattle of the Scotch Highlands." The influence of French manufacturers has extended even to the sheep husbandry of the southern hemisphere. As the fine combing-wool industry of France was extended, her own wools became insufficient to supply her looms. Regenerators of the Rambouillet stock were largely introduced into Australia, originally producing only clothing wools. The wools of Australia have becomelengthened in their fibre, and the exports of Australia, according to M. Moll, are now principally destined for the combing-wool industry.

The peculiar necessities of the French woollen industry have led to one of the most remarkable zootechnic achievements—and one which could not have been effected without the auspices of the manufacturer,—the creation of a new race of sheep and of an absolutely new fibre. The enormous prices of Cashmere shawls stimulated the French manufacturers in the early part of this century to emulate the Indian tissues. They succeeded perfectly in the fabrication. They induced, also, the importation of a large number of Cashmere goats, the animals furnishing down from which the Indian shawls are fabricated. It was found, however, that the goats could not be cultivated with profit, as each animal produced only three or four ounces of down. In 1828, there was accidentally produced at the farm of Mauchamp, cultivated by M. Graux, a ram of the merino race, which besides other peculiarities or monstrosities was provided with a wool remarkable for its softness, and above all for its lustre, which resembled that of silk. By a system of careful breeding, M. Graux succeeded in obtaining a small flock of animals from this stock whose wool was perfectly silky. He at first met with but little encouragement. The ordinary manufacturers, to whom he offered his wool, complained that it was so pliant and slippery that nothing could be done with it. Fortunately the silky wool attracted the attention of M. Davin, a wool manufacturer familiar with the fabrication of the Cashmere fibre, and distinguished for his zeal and skill in introducing new material into the textile arts. Taking the silky wool in hand, he succeeded in making magnificent stuffs which won the admiration of connoisseurs. Merinos, mousselines, satins of China, and shawls, made of this material, equalled, if they did not surpass, analogous products made of the finest Cashmere yarns. "The silky wool," says a report of the Imperial Society of Acclimation, "is destined to replace completely in our industry the Cashmere wool which comes from Thibet. It is fully as brilliant as Cashmere and as soft, while it costs less as a raw material, and requires less manipulation to be transformed to yarn."

The Mauchamp or silk-woolled race of sheep is now definitely established. I need not say that this beautiful creation could not have been effected in a country where the arts were not already developed to apply it.

The merino sheep, introduced into Germany about the same time as into France, received an improvement in an opposite direction. This direction was mainly given by the demands of the German wool manufacture, though partially due to a dry climate and unfruitful soil. Germany was already provided with sheep producing coarse clothing wool. They continued to suffice for the clothing of the great mass of the people, who were not elevated and wealthy as they have since become through the influence of the protective Zollverein, nor educated, as they have since been in Prussia, through the wise counsels of the immortal Humboldt. The early woollen manufacture of Germany was directed to the supply of cloths for the more wealthy classes. The combing-wool industry had been scarcely attempted. The first demand of the manufacture, therefore, was for fine clothing wools. The German flock-masters, being generally wealthy landholders, possessed the ability and intelligence to respond to this demand. The ideal in sheep husbandry became the production of the finest possible fibre. The ideal has been completely attained. The characteristic wools of Germany, those of the Electoral race, are much finer than those produced from the original Spanish stock; and the animals are much smaller in size, while the fleeces are correspondingly small. The extremely fine fibre, designated in Germany as *noble wool*, is marked by the distinctness and great number of its curves or wrinkles. The wools are distinguished not only for their fineness, but the extreme shortness of their staple, which give the felting qualities essential for the fine broadcloths and doeskins, for which German manufactures are so celebrated. These wools bear the highest price of any known, although the profitableness of their culture exclusively is questioned even in Germany. Still they form a leading source of German wealth. Eighteen per cent. of all the exports of wealthy Prussia consists of woollen manufactures, and those principally fine cloths. Thus we have a manufacturing industry acting directly upon agriculture; this reacting in its turn upon manufactures, until a distinct physiognomy is impressed upon the German national fabric, and the chief agricultural distinction of Germany has become that of possessing the most perfect fine-wool husbandry of the world.

Results quite different, but no less distinctive, have been effected by the influence of the woollen manufacture in the United States. Sheep husbandry in this country has been hitherto pursued exclusively with a view to the production of wool, mutton being a mere incident, and manure hardly a matter of consideration. The character of our sheep husbandry has, therefore, been wholly determined by the demand of manufacture. The American manufacturers have found it more profitable to run their mills upon the classes of goods in demand by the mass of our people. The masses of American consumers, although not demanding superfine cloths, require goods of a better and finer class than would content the masses of European population. Sound and sightly cloths, but of medium fineness, are in the greatest demand. Medium wools, produced by merino grades, of considerable length of fibre, are well suited to the production of flannels and fancy cassimeres, our principal products in the clothing-wool manufacture. It is true that the fine broadcloth manufacture was attempted under the fostering influence of the protective tariffs of 1824 and 1828, and was further extended under the tariff of 1842 ; and the culture of Saxony or superfine woolled sheep was pursued with enthusiasm. The horizontal tariff of 1846 destroyed the broadcloth manufacture, and at the same time swept away our Saxony sheep or merged them into coarser flocks. The demand for broadcloth wools having ceased, the American breeders of merinos, adapting themselves to the wants of manufactures, sought to produce a coarser and longer staple than had been in request at an earlier period. They have produced, through these influences, a race of sheep designated as the American merino and now recognized as a distinctive variety, like the Saxon merino or French merino. The most complete account of the American merino is the elaborate paper furnished to the report "On Wool and Manufactures of Wool," at the Paris Exposition, by Dr. Randall, the highest American authority on sheep husbandry, and no less favorably known as author of the Life of Jefferson. The remarkable improvement in productions of wool, effected by American husbandry upon the original Spanish stock, is the most interesting fact brought out in this excellent paper. From facts and experiments in scouring which he details, Dr. Randall says: "It appears, first, that prime American merinos produced more *washed* wool, in 1844–46, than was produced of unwashed wool by the original stock in Spain, at their palmiest period; second, that prime American merinos produce about as much scoured wool now as they did of washed wool in 1844–46, and nearly twice as much as the picked merino flock of the King of Great Britain from 1798 to 1802. They undoubtedly produce twice as much scoured wool as the average of the prime Spanish flocks of that period." By breeding to produce heavy fleeces, the wool of the American merino has become elongated so as to make it a true combing wool. No use of this quality has been made until very recently, except in delaines, a comparatively low fabric. The American Commissioner at the Paris Exposition, in the department of woollens, who, though largely interested in manufactures, had at that time but little practical experience in fabricating, was fascinated by the magnificent French merino fabrics at the Exposition. Upon his return to this country his attention was drawn to a fleece of American merino wool, which had been sent from Ohio to the office of the Association which I serve, to illustrate the combing qualities of the American staple. He instantly resolved to emulate in the mill of which he had the direction, with our merino combing wools, the French fabrics which he had admired abroad. Within less than two years the resolution has been crowned with complete success; his establishment has achieved several entirely new dress fabrics, made wholly of native fibre, such as had never been attempted in England, and at least three thousand pounds of American merino clothing wool are consumed per week in this new fabrication. This achievement I regard as *the* event in this year's history of the woollen industry of the United States. Perhaps I may be excused for recalling in this connection an intimation which I made in a published address five years ago: "The true value of the fleece of the American merino is for combing purposes, for which it has a remarkable analogy with that of France. This country will never know the inestimable treasure which it has in its fleeces until American manufacturers appropriate them to fabricate the soft tissues of merinos, thibets, and cashmeres, to which France owes the splendor of the industries of combing wool at Paris, Rheims, and Roubaix."

The relations of our industry with agriculture are so fascinating that they have too long detained me from the most important branch of my subject, — the relations of the wool manufacture to the higher arts and the other mechanical industries. As the oldest of textile arts, the woollen industry has filled the pages of history with illustrations of its civilizing influences. Passing by the voyage of the Argonauts for the golden fleece, and the fruits of that expedition, the birth of the arts of navigation and the origin of Phœnician letters, — a fable, indeed, but one teaching the same lesson which I would inculcate; passing by Tyre, enriched by the commerce of its murex-dyed tissues and fleeces; the Italian States, Florence, Venice, Pisa, and Genoa, which were the first in the twelfth and thirteenth centuries to appropriate the arts which the Crusaders brought back from Asia, and who found in the woollen manufacture the source of the wealth whose fruits survive in the "stones of Venice," and the wonders of Florentine art, for Michel Angelo's great statue of David was paid for by the wool-weavers' guild; passing by Flanders, where the growth of the wool manufacture and of Flemish art were contemporaneous, and which subsequently became the centre from which the art of fabricating woollens spread into England, France, and Germany,—turning aside from these brilliant examples, I would point you to a homely and familiar illustration at our own doors of the indirect influence of the woollen industry upon the sister arts.

Mr. Benton has pointed out with singular felicity the successive events which mark out the routes of the great railroad lines across the continent; first the path of the buffalo, then the Indian's, then the trapper's trail, then the emigrant's wagon and dawning civilization, and finally the railroad train, and civilization accomplished. Manufacturing industry has been established by a similar succession.

Settlements are made in the beginning upon our water courses. Water power is first applied to the saw-mill; then comes the grist-mill; then follows the woollen-mill: in old times it was the fulling-mill. The fulling-mill was, and the woollen-mill now is, to a matured industry, what the emigrant's wagon is to the great interior, the dawn of manufacturing enterprise, as that is of permanent settlement. The cotton, the machinery, the iron, the silk, the paper manufactures follow and build up our Lowells, Patersons, and Manchesters. This is no fancy sketch. I remember the time when the Salmon Falls River, watering a district which was occupied by one of the earliest and most important settlements in New England, dating back to 1632, had no other manufacturing establishments than a saw-mill, a grist-mill, and a fulling-mill. The latter disappeared, and was succeeded in 1828 by a well-appointed woollen factory. Afterwards came the cotton-mills of Great Falls; and the Salmon Falls River moves now one hundred and thirty-two thousand cotton spindles and fourteen sets of woollen machinery. This is but a type of the march of manufactures everywhere in this country. The first textile manufacturing establishment in Massachusetts was a fulling-mill, built at Rowley, near Ipswich, in 1643. This was the pioneer of a textile industry in Massachusetts, which, according to the Commonwealth returns in 1865, amounted to $144,730,679. The woollen-mills in the North-west, California, and Oregon, are in their turn the pioneers of a diversified industry in the newly settled States. The erection of a woollen mill of two or four sets seems to us at the East but a trifling affair, but to the new States it is an epoch, the dawn of manufactures, which all experience tells us will expand into a largely diversified industry and its attendant results, a superior civilization. The historian, Thiers, chronicles a more insignificant event than the building of a four-set mill, as an epoch in history. The introduction of a little manufacture of cloths, at Abbeville in France, by Colbert, is recorded as a more important conquest than that of his master, Louis XIV., who struck down the Spanish power. I have mentioned the fulling-mill as really the pioneer of the textile industry in this country. Few have a conception of the very brief period within which the woollen industry has attained its present development. A hundred years ago in England, and fifty years ago in this country, the woollen manufacture, as it now is, had hardly an existence. The spinning and weaving of wool was simply a domestic industry, power being used only in the fulling-mills. Dyer, despised by Dr. Johnson as poet, because his subject, the Fleece, partook of "the meanness naturally adhering to trade and manufactures," but now regarded as a better poet than the great critic, and also as the best annalist of the industry of his time, describes the manner in which the products of the woollen industry were collected, a century or more ago, for British commerce: —

"From little tenements by wood or croft,
Through many a slender path, how sedulous,
As rills to river broad, they speed their way
To public roads.
And thence explore,
Through every navigable wave, the sea,
That leaps the green earth 'round."

Some of our leading living wool manufacturers were apprenticed in their youth to clothiers, or the workers of the old fulling-mill; and one so apprenticed, from whom I recently sought reminiscences of the early manufacture, well remembers the farmers of Connecticut trudging miles through the woods with rolls of cloth upon their shoulders, to be felted and dressed in the fulling-mill. We sometimes regret the Arcadian days, when

> "Maids at the wheel, the weaver at the loom,
> Sat blithe and happy."

But considering the matter more practically, how vast an improvement upon this toilful and unproductive industry is that of the present time, when a single establishment, such as the Washington Mills, of Lawrence, Massachusetts, with its hundred sets, was capable, according to the statement of its late lamented treasurer, Mr. Stetson, by working day and night, to produce all the woollen clothing for an army of a million men.

Let me give the relations of the woollen manufacture to particular textile arts, and first to the cotton manufacture. The cotton manufacture of Great Britain, the most stupendous phenomenon of modern industry, was the natural offshoot of the woollen manufacture. Through the woollen trade, mainly, England had become a nation of spinners and weavers, or of artisans subsidiary to them. A national taste and skill had been developed in the textile arts by the manipulation of wool, which was readily applicable to a kindred fibre. Many of the inventions upon which the cotton manufacture is dependent, such as the invention of the fly-shuttle, which doubled the power of the weaver and made necessary the subsequent inventions which increased the spinning power, were contributed directly from the seats of the woollen manufacture. What was scarcely less important, the commercial connections established by the woollen trade gave to the cotton manufacture, when completely inaugurated by the inventions of Hargreaves, Arkwright, and Compton, a command of foreign markets for unlimited exports of the new British textile. The British cotton manufacture is as truly the offspring of the woollen industry as New England is of Old England. This may be called the most important incident of the woollen industry; for in giving birth to that of cotton, it secured to England, from the fabrication of that textile, a profit in fifty years of *one thousand million pounds sterling*. Pursue these consequences still further, and we have the cotton gin in America, the growth of the slave power, its aggressions, the war of the rebellion, and emancipation!

The cotton manufacture, reaching maturity, discharged its filial debt by giving an unexpected and singular development to the woollen industry.

Between 1830 and 1840, cotton became an important auxiliary to wool, through its use in warps for woollen or worsted filling in the fabrication of tissues for female wear. Many varieties of these union fabrics are classed under the generic name of cotton delaines. This fabric was first introduced into France in 1833, and into England in 1834. It is practically the same as a woollen fabric, the warps being so covered with wool that the presence of cotton can be observed only by the closest inspection. Its cheapness, durability, and sightliness, when printed, make its introduction an invaluable boon to women of moderate means. Not less than sixty thousand yards are annually manufactured in this country, and the cheapness and excellence of the American fabric practically excludes its foreign rivals. The cotton warps are now used as vehicles to extend the surface of wool and worsted mohair and alpaca in a countless variety of dress fabrics. The wool of a single sheep may be extended by the cotton warp so as to fabricate 672 yards of so-called alpaca fabrics, enough for fifty-six dresses. All the cheaper fabrics are made by this wholly modern alliance of wool and cotton, and the great manufacturing cities of Bradford, in England, and Roubaix, in France, are chiefly occupied in the fabrication of these cheap tissues, whose undoubted fragility is rendered less objectionable by the fickleness of female fashion.

An establishment producing fabrics of this class will give us the best illustration of the manifold and important relations of the woollen industry of the present period. I select the establishment known as the Pacific Mills, located at Lawrence, Massachusetts, because it is the oldest and largest of its class. This establishment turns out an annual product of printed delaines and calicoes, principally the former, valued at not less than $7,500,000. In the production of its union fabrics the mill works up each year thirty-five hundred thousand pounds of fleece wool or the fleeces of ten thousand sheep each week. For washing this wool it makes and consumes annually two hundred and fifty thousand pounds of soap, composed by the domestic products, lard and caustic soda. It combines with this wool, in the form of cotton warps, thirty-five hundred thousand pounds of cotton. In the processes of spinning and weaving it expends twelve thousand gallons of lubricating oils and ten thousand gallons of olive oil. The raw materials for dyeing and printing, such as soda ash, sulphur, prussiates of potash, the various preparations of tin, the dyewoods, indigo, cochineal, yellow berries, and aniline colors, &c., require an annual expenditure of $400,000. The consumption of potato starch is five hundred tons a year, or the product of one hundred and twenty-five thousand bushels of potatoes. $30,000 a year is expended in lumber and nails for packing boxes, an expenditure which, in twenty years, would build up a considerable town. As much more is expended annually in iron, steel, lumber, and paints for repairs; fourteen thousand tons of coal are consumed yearly, although the motive power of the mill is water. To this may be added the food and clothing of thirty-six hundred operatives aud of their dependants, at least twice as many more, and the items of transportation of raw material and manufactured products. Considering these multiform relations, how vast is the wave of production set in motion by the wheels of a single mill, and how broadly extended are its ever-enlarging circles; for the materials of consumption above enumerated show that the productive stimulus of this industrial centre moves labor, not only in fields of the South and the pastures of the West, but in the plains of India, the forests of Brazil, and the islands of the equator.

The wool manufacture makes itself auxiliary to other textile arts, as to those of linen and silk. The flax or linen manufacture is particularly allied to that of wool in the production of Brussels and tapestry carpets. A single Brussels carpet factory, producing five hundred and fifty thousand yards of carpeting, consumes annually a quantity of linen warps of the value of $150,000. Another establishment, making principally tapestry, Brussels, and velvet carpets, to the extent of eight hundred and eighteen thousand yards, besides thirty thousand yards of Brussels, consumed for the filling and backs 793,866 pounds of linen yarn and jute, costing $167,000, besides two hundred and two thousand pounds of cotton yarn for warps, costing $90,000.

The silk manufacture is an important contributor to the woollen industry. One form of the alliance of silk and wool is the silk poplin, the warp being of long combing wool and the weft of silk. This tasteful, though useful fabric, is now largely produced in Connecticut and New Jersey, and the American production compares favorably with the celebrated poplins of Ireland. Another form of this alliance is the silk-warped flannel, now produced in our mills in connection with the manufacture of the beautiful opera flannels, formerly brought exclusively from France.

The most important form is the silk-mixed Cassimere, the alliance of silk with merino wool, through the infinite combinations made by our Crompton mule-producing fabrics, distinguished for their subdued lustre, and the softness of their neutral tints. A single manufacturing house of your city, whose silk and wool mixtures are admitted to vie with those of Elbœuf, and which, as I shrewdly suspect, the dealers, not the manufacturers, usually sell as such, consumes annually $150,000 worth of American silk organzine. The whole amount of silk consumed by our mills is estimated by good authority at not less in value than a million dollars.

I can barely refer to two other very important industries, one of which is directly in one department, and the other mainly founded upon our wool manufacture, — the manufacture of hats and that of ready-made clothing. The former, in one of its branches,—that of wool hats, and in the first part of its processes, the preparation of raw material, — is really a branch of the wool manufacture. It is too important a branch not to be referred to, as the annual production of wool hats in the United States exceeds in value ten million dollars. The industry of ready-made clothing, dating back no further than 1824, and now the most important single one of our city industries, obtains its supply of material substantially from the American wool manufacture. The official statistics of Massachusetts for 1865 show that this industry in the city of Boston alone yielded a production of $15,186,833, and employed fourteen hundred and seventy-nine males and nineteen thousand, two hundred and five females. If the production in the other cities is in the same proportion, the part which the offspring plays in supporting American labor is scarcely less important than that of the parent industry.

I have not time to trace the relations of the woollen manufacture to the chemical arts, nor to follow in any detail the progress of discovery from the period of the great impulse given by Colbert, who, in introducing the woollen manufacture into France, made improvement in the art of dyeing the object of special care, considering, as he happily says, " dyeing as the soul of tissues, without which the body could hardly exist." The discovery of Prussian blue in 1704, of chromium in the latter part of the century, the fixing of color by means of steam in 1810, the application to union fabrics in 1857, the discovery of alizarine in 1826, of murexide, the reproduction of the Tyrian dye in 1856, of aniline dyes from coal tar in the same year, and finally the most brilliant chemical discovery of the last two years, that of producing from coal tar the coloring principle of madder, alizarine, —a discovery of such practical value that the product of the coal fields is already replacing the product of the madder fields among the Scotch dyers. Most of these discoveries have had their impulse, as the great industries which supply the materials for dyeing have their support, in the textile arts, and principally in the woollen industry, which makes the largest application of color.

I must hasten to my final illustration; the relations of the woollen manufacture to the industries producing machinery. In this view I do not regard of chief importance the many special industries directly and exclusively employed in constructing machinery and supplies for our mills, although the capital and labor which they employ make them worthy of more than a passing notice. A few establishments construct all the classes of machinery made use of in our mills. But generally the work is divided. Some build only pickers, others carding machines, others jacks, others looms, others shears. Others make supplies for both woollen and cotton mills, as card clothing, reeds, harnesses, shuttles, bobbins, spools, and belting. The bare enumeration shows how important is this direct relation of the woollen manufacture. But I desire in closing to call your attention to a broader view, and therefore will not separate the woollen manufacture from the other textile arts of which it was the pioneer.

The textile industries of the wool and cotton made, in England during the last century, the first extended application of the new motor power, steam, which, for some time after its appearance, had been condemned to a sort of obscurity by being applied only to the drainage of mines. The power of steam was first made *conspicuous* by the woollen and cotton mills. The factory system and the movement of textile machinery by power demanded the construction of great numbers of pieces of machinery of the same dimensions, and also the construction of works of nice mechanism, which the mere hand-craftsmen, the whitesmiths of a former age, could not supply in sufficient number, nor with the requisite precision of construction. Machine shops were, therefore, erected upon a large scale, to be moved by power. It is well known that the great machine shops of this country arose contemporaneously with the factories in Providence, Lowell, and Philadelphia. The necessities of the textile manufactures, then, and for the first time, called into existence the automatic mechanical contrivances called machine tools and engines ; the planers and lathes and steam hammers which substitute the firm, *iron arm* for the weak and uncertain human hand,—contrivances which have caused the disappearance, in the manufacturing world at least, of the file, the plane, the chisel, the auger, the drill, in the hand of man, except for the most trivial and unimportant purposes. The power and accuracy of constructive art were thus marvellously extended. Masses of iron of thirty or forty tons' weight are wrought and transformed with more facility and in less time than a bar of a few hundreds' weight could have been fifty years ago. The precision of construction attained is so perfect, according to President Barnard, the chief ornament of the science of your city, who has suggested much which I have just said, that the dimensions of a required piece of work may be gauged to the one-millionth part of an inch. The machine tools, created by and for the textile manufactures, were now ready for new applications. River and lake steamboats, locomotives, ocean steamers, monitors, appeared in succession, the methods of interior transportation are revolutionized, and the entire naval marine, and almost entire commercial marine of the world are completely transformed. In all the manufacturing nations, and particularly in our own, a passion for invention has been developed with the new facilities for putting in practice the conceptions of inventive power. The arts succeed each other by a true generation. Idea begets idea, and the invention of to-day gives birth to the invention of to-morrow. In the genial atmosphere of invention new industries take root in the old, like epiphytes in the humid forests of the tropics. Watchmaking by machinery was established at Waltham, the cradle of the cotton manufacture in Massachusetts; and a still more luxurious art, the working of silver plate by machinery, was founded at Providence, the birthplace of the cotton manufacture of Rhode Island.

For a long time the mechanical arts reacted chiefly upon each other. The inventive and constructive power invoked by manufactures reached tardily, but at length, the fields of husbandry. The labor-saving machinery of the farm, the harvesters, reapers, mowers, and planters of the last two decades, came into existence. Agriculture, now doubled in its productive capacity, not by improvements properly its own, but through the auxiliary forces of the mechanical arts, presents the final and triumphant demonstration of the solidarity of the industries. This is the idea which called into existence your noble Institute, which inspires the grand expositions that distinguish the present age, and which you have made so obvious to our senses by placing the dahlia, the grape cluster, and the wheat sheaf by the side of the organ, the engine, and the loom, and by gathering all these fair products of labor under the self-supporting carpentry of this vast dome, which is thus an emblem of the unity of national industry.

www.ingramcontent.com/pod-product-compliance
Lightning Source LLC
LaVergne TN
LVHW011139110826
845150LV00008B/2420
* 9 7 8 1 4 1 8 1 9 3 1 7 1 *